POSSIBLE

DREAM THE IMPOSSIBLE

AVIT BANSAL

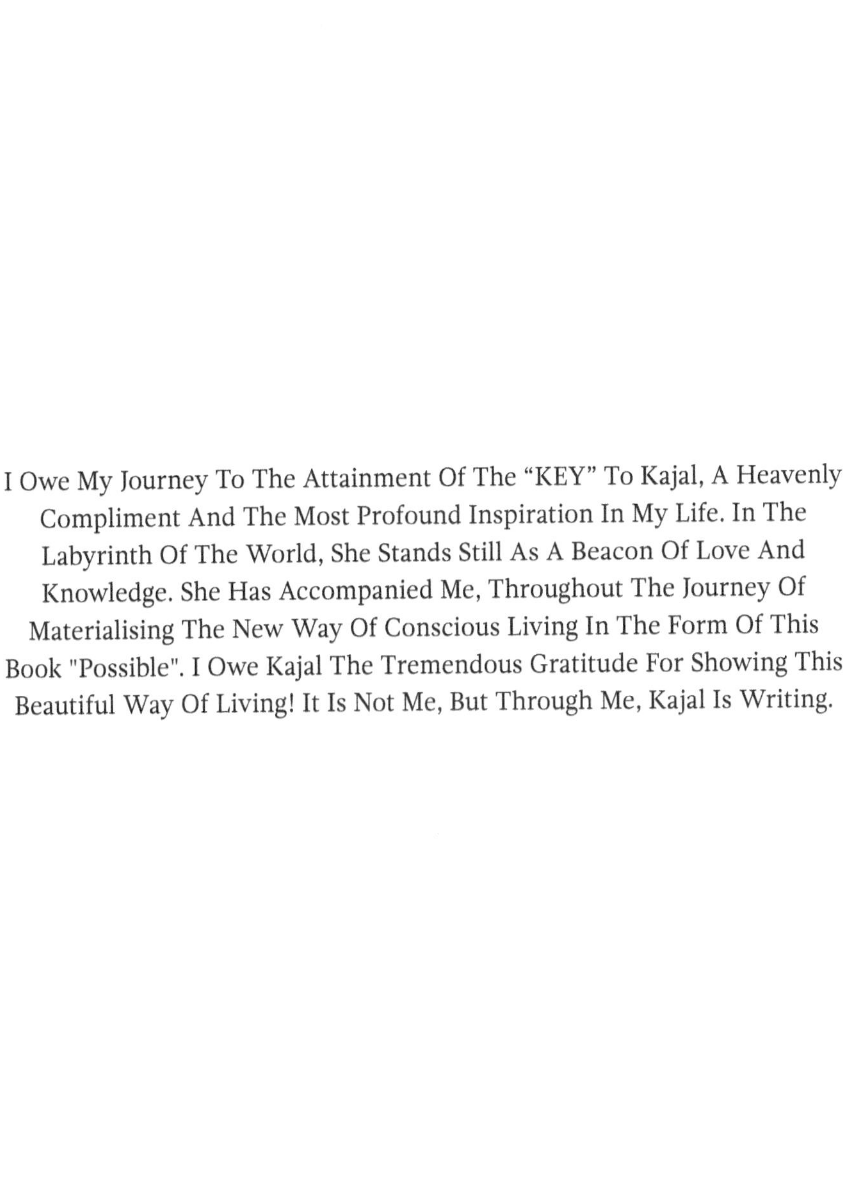

I Owe My Journey To The Attainment Of The "KEY" To Kajal, A Heavenly Compliment And The Most Profound Inspiration In My Life. In The Labyrinth Of The World, She Stands Still As A Beacon Of Love And Knowledge. She Has Accompanied Me, Throughout The Journey Of Materialising The New Way Of Conscious Living In The Form Of This Book "Possible". I Owe Kajal The Tremendous Gratitude For Showing This Beautiful Way Of Living! It Is Not Me, But Through Me, Kajal Is Writing.

Contents

POSSIBLE

ix

Dream The Impossible

In Hope To Wake You Up

CHAPTER ONE

THE HARDEST PART

""The hardest part is starting. Once you get out of the way, you will find rest of the journey much easier" -Simon Sinek"

Imagine, yes imagine! confronting a radical thinker and making him realize that he was wrong, in his beliefs, he made wrong assumptions his whole life. Just like telling a priest or a religious figure that he prayed to the wrong god his whole life. There is a good chance that he won't give his two cents to you, no matter what proof, living or dead you may provide. This was always the case, you may refer to the time when the geocentric approach was negated, the times when the "ones" who challenged the established beliefs, were taught the dear lessons. Let's not dwell on the details of each such instances. It would be better to accept, the longer the belief is held, the harder it is to change. Now let's bring those times to now, what if I say, to you all, the readers, are living life the "not so supposed" way! Don't worry, I have no enmity towards you but for the sake of the argument, let's assume this situation. You praised and followed the wrong ideals, you were always told the "lies". You are the fruit of the tree that was fed on misconceptions of life, you were the students of the teacher, who didn't know the depth of the subject, the subject which you mastered. Who "AM I" to preach to you, that you were all wrong, your mastery of the subject is all but the reality! The assumptions and ideals that you wore so close to your bones are deeply infused within you and form an integral part of your nature and personality. Let us come to the hard part now. For a moment, suppose, I have a "KEY", "KEY" which opens any door, which life allows, has or might have. Which could be a door to healthy relationships, material success, abundance, happiness or any door you want to access, you think it, you have it. But there is a catch! For the "KEY", you must trade, yes! you need to trade it dearly. If you can trade dearly, you can have the "KEY" which allows you to pass any door, which life offers. What is the trade then? one might ask. You need to trade all of YOU, all your beliefs, all your ideals, all your limiting beliefs, you need to let go of your OLD SELF, you need to be re-born in this world, and you need to start afresh! Will you trade? Or will you not give two cents just like the radical thinker? For a radical thinker, this would be a textbook, for a trader it would be itself a "KEY"!

""It's not the LEARNING, it's the UNLEARNING, which is tough""

Let's make one thing very clear, it is the good that comes to the trader to be traded, not the other way around. In this case, the GOOD(Possible), came to you(Trader), not the other way around. This is the gist of the "Possible". You might not understand it yet completely, but we will together dwell on its meaning in forthcoming chapters.

* * *

CHAPTER TWO

THE "KEY"

The "KEY" has always been the way of life, just like law, like any other law, the law of Gravity. You cannot escape it, you were, are and will be subject to it. Whether you notice or not, the KEY doesn't need your approval for its existence or its operation. It is the way of life. Do not take my word for it, by the end of this book traders will trade it dearly, you will understand it, feel it and most importantly will see it and implement it. Again, the KEY is under no obligation to your acceptance for its existence, It is universal and a LAW. KEY is not a physical thing, it's merely an epiphany. The epiphany which changes your life, if you are a trader. Usually, a trader wants to trade his money with the goods he intends to buy. The GOOD represents his desire, desire could be - his intention to get the riches of the world, the fame of the world, the relationship of the world, a cure for illness and the intention never stops. Here you are the TRADER, the readers, and desires could be a better job, a better lifestyle, a better relationship, a better house, maybe. Now the question arises, are you willing to trade the KEY for your GOODS/Desires? But for your desires, you need to trade everything you have, all the riches you have. There should be no money left unspent in your pocket, you need to give each penny including the lint of your pocket, lint means the doubts. The Traders who are willing to go "All in" should and would get KEY, and must read the epiphany of the KEY, for the Traders lurking in the back, would feel like bystanders of the auction and should feel this as a textbook only.

"So, Are You Willing to Trade?"

Dear, Traders, now it's time to drop all your belongings here, any baggage that you might be having! Put all the preconceived notions, beliefs, notions and your ego here. There is no need for them, from this point forward. You don't need to build a new house using old bricks! The house built in such a way, does not last and crumbles with the slightest burden of doubts. You don't put fresh wine in an old flask! You don't dress the wound with old dressings. What do I mean by this? Simply, put your beliefs and thoughts that have gained throughout your long life, here. Just like removing your sandals before entering the sanctum sanctorum of the temple. Let all the knowledge that you have dearly collected, throughout your life, drop down here. Let's be "with nothing on" from here onwards. Let's do the "ablution" of your thoughts. Let's be white in all senses. On your way to return, you will have your chance to pick them up once again. But again, the KEY is under no obligation to make sense to you, just like a stream of water is under no obligation to you. It will "FLOW", even if you turn your eyes away from it. You can close your eyes, mute your ears, and get miles away from it. It will still flow.

"Now, Whenever you are ready!"

* * *

CHAPTER THREE

ORIGIN

"There are no accidents, just the things we don't yet perceive!"

Do you really believe that you, the complex being, are sent here, on earth, without purpose? Think again!, is it all just random sequences of events which brought us here? With the degree of complexity, can we question our origin? Even our consciousness? Think again! Don't take my word for it! Think again!

Look around you, and observe your environment. Think again! Ask yourself "WHO AM I?" Ask again, and again and again till you detach from the environment and really grasp the nature of your question. Don't stop, the more sincerely you ask yourself the closer you will get to the answer, it's the only question in the entire existence, which answers itself. The more you ask, the closer you will get to the answer. Sit down, keep aside this book and close your eyes if you prefer, and sincerely ask, "WHO AM I".

For the answer of "WHO AM I?" the great sages and religious figures of our times, spent their entire lives living in solitude, Great Budhha spent and wandered years and years for the search of the same. Just to find that the answer lies in plain sight. Ever heard, the best place to hide the secret is in plain sight? Gautama Buddha, on attainment of enlightenment, laughed incessantly knowing that the answer was in front of him, all these times. It was the efforts of those sage-like figures which helped humanity to find the answer for "WHO AM I?", just like it took Edison, a multitude of efforts to give us the answer for darkness, the Light Bulb. Newton took years of solitude to give us laws of motion and Gravity. Now, let's suppose you built a sandcastle, and there you made a sandman. One fortunate day, the sandman stood up and started to ponder about "its" existence, and started to think about the material "it" is made of. We are the same, we are the part of the universe, made up of the universal materials, and atoms, and pondering about our existence. We are no different from the sandman contemplating his existence. It's that essence that gave Sandman to contemplate his existence, which is the answer to the question "WHO AM I?". It may be the most simplified explanation of the answer. So what's the answer to the question "WHO AM I?", ask yourself, after noticing the sandman. To simply put, its awareness of being! Which you might know as a concept of consciousness, it's the same awareness of being which made the sandman ponder. And it's the same essence for which Gautama Buddha laughed about, it's the same essence, which is the answer to the question "WHO AM I?". We are awareness of being! We are consciousness. We are the sandman in a sandcastle, we are a part of the universe, experiencing itself. I could have given you all the literature of the world to explain to you the concept of awareness of being or so as to call "CONSCIOUSNESS". Which would be futile at this stage. The world is full of knowledge, one can reach the end of his life to answer the question "WHO AM I?" Re-read the above SANDMAN and SANDCASTLE given above, maybe a few more times, now one last time! Maybe we are not so different from that SANDMAN! Just as the sandman got aware of its being, it was conscious of its being. Having made up of the same elements as of the SANDCASTLE. Which could imply, CASTLE is also aware of its being, because SANDMAN is made up of the same elements as that of castle, Let's call this the higher consciousness. SANDCASTLE , having higher consciousness, is encompassing the SANDMAN having the Consciousness. The Higher Consciousness is connected to the Consciousness by virtue of its origin and nature, that is, SANDMAN being the part of SANDCASTLE. This same correlation represents our relationship with the universe, us, having the Consciousness , is the part of a higher consciousness, that of the universe. Some might call it GOD, some might call it the universe, some might call it by their preferred name of religious GODs, It's all the same. We are just part of a higher consciousness. Higher awareness of being. Every religion points to one thing, some sort of higher power, some energy, some awareness of being. Right from the oldest to the newest religions, all mention the Higher one! the higher power.

"WHO AM I? I AM THAT I AM"

We are the awareness, consciousness that is the part of higher consciousness. You might find its resonance, from biblical references, we are made in a godlike image, not only bible but many mystic, esoteric teachings, hinduism, buddhism all made references to the same, which got diluted in course of time. For the sake of defining the concept of Consciousness , we can go on and on, filling pages, but my motive here is to make you aware, yes aware! About the simplicity of the answers you were looking for "Creating life". The life which you always wanted. For now, we can say we are consciousness, and a part of greater consciousness. Let's do one simple exercise, let's sit down quietly in a comfortable position, or in a yogic position. Now let your mind run wild, let's go with the flow, soon you might find yourself drifting away in your thoughts, your mind will drag you away in winds of the thoughts, might be a thought of getting next promotion, might be a thought of attending the kid's seminar, might be thought of embarrassment from your past or a worry from the future, it could be anything. For the creative minds and overthinkers - some imaginary utopian or self-induced thought would be there, but one thing is for sure, there would be a constant wind of thoughts. Continuing the same exercise, now, let's focus on what kinds of thoughts you are having, just don't react, notice what's going on in your mind carefully and objectively as a third person or as an innocent bystander. Sit quietly and just observe what kind of thoughts you are having. Now one may notice, as soon as you start to notice your thoughts, the thoughts would start to disappear or start to get interrupted. But Why? Let's do this once again and notice it carefully. One crucial question arises here, if the mind, so-called brain - is itself creating thoughts then who/what is that "thing", which is observing the thoughts? You may try this exercise many times over, and think who/what is that, noticing our thoughts? That's your consciousness! The exercise we did, forms the basis of meditation. The "thing" observing your thoughts is your awareness of being. This would be the most basic explanation of the concept of Consciousness. The contemporary scientific community, is yet to conclude the nature and definition of consciousness concretely. But from what we can see, spiritualism is the only discipline which has defined consciousness, the awareness of being with full confidence, the SCIENCE is yet to touch it. And in my perspective, with current mindset and limited tools, the SCIENCE will never get to the conclusive answer. Our understanding of the universe is limited because the parameters on which we deduce conclusion in scientific community is not at par to understand the complex nature of the universe, we are still using our limited 3D minds to understand multidimensional nature of the universe.The Quantum physics has made an bold attempt to understand the multidimensional nature of the universe.

The story of SANDMAN and SANDCASTLE can be taken once again to understand the relational nature of SANDMAN and SANDCASTLE, or in our case, the universe and us. All the metaphysics teachers emphasized the interconnected nature of our universe, which science is slowly catching on the same. The Quantum entanglement is a great START to understand the interconnectedness of the universe, which again implies the interconnectedness of the whole universe. This interconnectedness of the universe has led certain esoteric followers to coined the term, "Matrix" or "Simulation". The proponents of the same argue we are living the simulation just like a software but at a universal level, and there exists a programmer who/who is controlling everything. Let's not get into the modern day speculation of the very nature of our "KEY". The one and ONLY goal of this book is to make you AWARE of your own power to live life in your desired own way.

Again, the sole motive of this book is only to make you AWARE of the fundamental facts of life, which is not what it seems to be, not at all what science thinks it is. Science is helpful in deducing the 3D world observations, yet again on confronting the multi dimensional nature of the world, the SCIENCE, remains silent or speculative. The senses which have, vision, touch, smell, taste and sense of hearing are evolved to perceive the tangible nature of our 3 dimensional reality. One living by them, senses the concrete nature of our reality. We are bound by 3 dimensional reality, as long as we stick to them. There is one more sense, which transcends the 3 dimensional reality and way beyond, it's our wonderful IMAGINATION. Which knows no boundary, no time or space. It cannot be contained, you may close your eyes and teleport yourself in a distant part of the world with blink on an eye. But the question arises, what is IMAGINATION and why are we gifted with it? What's the purpose of this sense of IMAGINATION? We can IMAGINE our victory or defeat, our love and hatred. Every Sense has its own purpose, but what about IMAGINATION? Just for daydreaming? Or does it have some purpose way beyond our understanding? Let's deep dive it in forthcoming chapters.

"Imagination is more important than Knowledge - Albert Einstein"

* * *

CHAPTER FOUR

UNCONSCIOUS LIVING

"WAKE UP!
It's the time for those who have been sleeping!"

You heard it right, it's the time for the readers, or must I say, the Traders to wake up. You have been sleeping your whole life, which brought you living in this moment. Look around you, the state which you are in, the dwelling in which you are affixed, the state of mind, the lifestyle you have, the life you have, you brought yourself here, and no one else. I have no enmity towards the TRADERS, but the traders must understand, they themselves brought, to this very moment of their own existence. There was no one other than themselves.

"Look what you've done!"

You are not a victim of the world, you are the doer of the things done unto you. Don't despise the messenger! The delivery man of this news, despise your state of sleepiness. You have been sleeping your whole life. Let's count the problems, which haunts us! Be it may - relationship, finances, career and the list goes on and goes, make a list of the things you are not happy about. I would really like the TRADERS to make a list of the problems they have been facing. Shyness or hesitation won't help. Remember, you came here "with nothing on ".

"Make a list! There is no other way around!"

If it would help, the list could contain phrases like - "I do not have the job of my dream", 'My familial relations are not good", "I don't feel worthy enough", "My finances are not good", "I always fail in my new ventures", "My specific person relationship is not working". Don't stop here, add any number of problems you have. Now box all the problems into one category - "DESIRE". The opposite of these problems which you are facing are your desires. Opposite of "I do not have the job of my dream" is "I have my dream job", 'My familial relations are not good" is "I have good familial relationships", "I don't feel worthy enough" is "I worthy of the goods and greetings", "My finances are not good" is "I have an abundance of wealth", "I always fail in my new ventures" is "I'm successful in my own ventures", "My specific person relationship is not working" is "Im in loving relation with my specific person". Now you have boxed them into one category of "DESIRES".

Let me state a fact! For which I won't blame you for not understanding "You are the roadblock on the way to your desires". Ask a few kids, (6-10 years old), about their dream home, and ask the same from a grown-up individual (25-30 years old), and again from mature adults (45+ years). Did you observe a pattern? What did you notice? Let me help you, the dream house of the innocent kid would be a colourful house, with a playhouse, with all the material fancy of the world, the things the kid would enjoy. It has no limitation, just pure DESIRE of the kid. This is what we call a PURE DESIRE, unhindered, unadulterated, the heart element in the desire of the kid is at maximum and the brain element is non-existent. A kid's desire is the heart's desire. Now for the early mature people, the house would be somewhat, what you may call "realistic", but would have a "dream" angle to it. Maybe a big lawn, a big estate with a pool. The dream is still resonating in their desires. The heart element is there, but the brain element has crept in. Now for the Mature individuals, the heart element is down to non-existent, they would tell you the last details of the house they want and would have a very restrictive dream element to it. The answers may vary, but the generalistic trend would be the PURE DESIRE, which has no brain element to it would decrease as we grow older. As we grow older, we start restricting our desires, which start becoming adulterated and brain elements start increasing. We start shutting the door on what our heart desires and allows what our brain thinks. The poor heart helplessly breaks down under the whims of the BRAIN! Now lets understand what a heart element and brain element is and how it works. Heart is your real desire, that you really want and Brain is your logical mind reducing your real and pure desire as per its understanding and limitations.

Heart: I want a Bungalow!

Brain: Okay! But that would cost around a Million bucks! We don't have that!

Heart: Okay then let's have a Million bucks!

Brain: Not possible! For that, you need to have a stable business or a good occupation.

Heart: Okay! So then let's have a stable business, we need that bungalow!

Brain: Not possible, the market competition in the business domain is too much, we cannot risk and neither do we have any capital for the business.

Heart: Oh! How can we have the money then to start the business and get our bungalow?

Brain: We need to do a job for at least 5 years to save the money to start the business.

Heart: Okay, Let's do it!

Brain: Not possible! The prices of the bungalow will skyrocket by then and then we need to buy our daily needs, and inflation is rising, I don't think we will be able to buy the bungalow, but maybe after 5 years, we can have a 2 BHK small cosy home on loan and interest.

Heart: But I want a bungalow!

Brain: Not possible!

Heart: Okay...

As one may notice, the Heart element represents our true desire and the brain element represents the limits on the same with myriads of reasonings over it. Brain element is simply just our thoughts and assumptions of the world. Which in turn suppressors our truest of true desires. As one grows older, the mindset shifts towards the brain element thus by suppressing the heart element. The greatest massacre done by mankind is the killing of the inner child, done unto itself. To test the same, have an inner conversation of the truest of desire, one may even find it difficult to find their true DESIRE because it has already been suppressed by the brain element, But! Where does this brain element come from? We keep collecting these from our past and experiences which finally accumulate to being a "Limiting belief". These limiting beliefs, when supported by our own thoughts, dissect our true desire into smaller comprehensible dreams , dissecting our heart and its desires. You can itself notice this by tracking your dreams growing up, it kept on growing dark and finally shelled into a remote dream. I dare the TRADERS to even think of their true desire, as soon as you try, the Brain element will jump in and thus limiting beliefs. These beliefs are often dressed to us by society and parenting as we grow up - "Good things are hard earned", "You need to put in hard work to earn money", "Nowadays good relationships are hard to come by", "Not all can do business and create a big empire".Notice how many times have you heard them in your childhood and growing up. Knowingly and unknowingly we keep them alive in our mind and self-talk thus allowing the limiting beliefs to get hold over us and thus killing our inner child and its PURE desire. In this way, a certain limiting belief becomes so engrossed in our subconscious mind that it starts directing our behaviour and shifts our goal completely from our DESIRES.

Look above the conversation between Heart and Brain, it all started with a PURE desire of a Bungalow and ended up towards working a job and getting a small cosy home. Now the person starts striving for the job to be maintained and a home on loans and interest. Let's set aside a few moments for ourselves, sit quietly and contemplate the number of desires you have killed in your own life for the meagre dreams which you are chasing, the dream which is not even yours! Carefully examine your life and list down your dreams and how you have broken them into smaller, non-valuable dreams. The way you live your life up till now is the result of being sleeping, so WAKE UP! You have been dreaming your whole life, collecting limiting beliefs and acting according to them, we have been mere zombies of our minds and thoughts! Yes, we are not victims of fate or of the world, we are doers of our own thoughts and Imagination! TRADERS, you have been living your life unconsciously. Which led you to the exact moment, NOW! Look around you, you are residing in the cradle which you made yourself. Let this be your wake-up call, let this be the "KEY", to it. You have been dreaming up till now, which you call the reality, now you must wake up to the "REAL REALITY".

* * *

CHAPTER FIVE

THE KEY - UNVEILED

"Do not think what you do not want!"

Conjure your ears and eyes for the words and wisdom of the KEY! We humans are gifted with the consciousness of being, which the sages of our past times have been focusing on. Which ultimately got reflected in dogmas and teachings of various esoteric as well as religious teachings. Numerous texts throughout history repeated the wisdom of the KEY, with different explanations just like the GRAVITY, which always existed but with time the explanation of which changed, the reasoning of the scientific community will change in future too, but the GRAVITY will remain so. Classical mechanics, modern mechanics and now quantum mechanics all have different explanations of the term GRAVITY but the phenomenon remains the same. The apple will always fall, irrespective of the change in the understanding of gravity. The KEY was, is and will be the same, it doesn't require anyone's consent for its operation, for it is a law. The biblical scriptures pointed to the same again and again but with the advent of time, the meaning got adulterated. Following time, again and again, the esoteric teachers revived it. Some may call it the law of attraction, some may call it the law of vibration, some may call it the law of assumption, and some may call it the modern-day term "Manifestation". In future, some quantum explanation will come up in which quantum entanglement is the precursor.

"We live through not, by so-called our actions, but by our thoughts and Imagination, called desires."

The KEY

Look around and pick anything up from your surroundings, anything man-made, was once in the imagination of the consciousness of a MAN. Right from the chair you are sitting in, to the food you are eating. Take your time and dwell in the thought. Let it be a simplistic needle to the complicated quantum computer. All was once just a Thought and Imagination. Every discovery ever made, every story ever written, every song which was ever sung, was first in the imagination! For the things which are not man-made was once in the imagination of our higher consciousness of the universe for which we call GOD. Creation is the fundamental nature of the consciousness. The higher consciousness created the entire universe including us. And imparted us the precious pearl, the sublet of higher consciousness, that is human consciousness. And as the nature of consciousness, we create not by physical actions but by imagination. We are bound to the creative nature of our consciousness. And the surrounding we dwell in is the by-product of our imagination and assumptions. For a man taught "the world is a place of suffering", suffering becomes inevitable. There is no one to blame, but us, no one to reward but us. A thief only sees the house with no locks, a carpenter sees the unfixed wood, a doctor sees only unhealed ailments, and a scientist only sees the laws of nature. What do you see? *"हम जैसा दखे ये जहा हैं वैसा ही"* a line from a beautiful song from the Bollywood movie, Taare Zameen par, perfectly resonates with the nature of the world. Meaning - The world is exactly what we imagine it to be, It's the tint or shade of spectacle you are wearing, which determines the colour of the world. The interesting thing to notice is that this shade or tint is not made by us, but rather imposed on us by our experiences and opinions which we have integrated through the world. We were never told about our imagination and power of consciousness, our dreams were hunted down in our childhood making consciousness idle. Throughout life, a man is imposed with the ideas, which MAN considers its own and true, which are no less than an illusion imposed by the world. MAN along with its consciousness has become the destroyer of desires instead of becoming a creator. Think of your heart's desire and let the mind run over it, it will be reduced to mere a fantasy and long distant reduced dream, because this is how we have evolved during our growing up. The reason, seclusion helped the sages and scientists because it helped their imagination grow without the impedance of worldly opinions and dictates.

"We are jailed by our imagination, and freedom lies in the same. Imagination and Faith are secrets of creation - Neville Goddard."

Everything celestial was once in the consciousness of our Higher, the universe, for which we are created in the godlike image, receiving the child of that consciousness, our wonderful human consciousness. For which we are sons of the Father (Universe). For which we are, our consciousness, is part of the higher consciousness of the universe. We have inherited the quality of being creators in our own world, Through our consciousness. But due course of time we have forgotten that we are creators through our imagination of our consciousness. We are lost and begotten. The material world, in which we dwell has engulfed us to the extent of being beggars instead of being creators. For the same reason, Indian culture refers to the world as being "MAYA", that is, the ILLUSION. Which simply reflects the reflection of our inner world, our consciousness. Knowingly, unknowingly, we are living our lives, bound by imagination and consciousness in a sleep. The "unaware" ones, of this fact, live their life within the bounds of their limiting beliefs. The "aware" ones, of this fact, create the life they wanted. We are bound by our imagination, thoughts and consciousness, so if one thinks the world is cruel, he will see nothing less than cruelty, if one thinks the world is full of love, he will see nothing less than love. There is an adage "Stay Positive" for a reason.

* * *

CHAPTER SIX

DESIRES – OUR ONLY PURPOSE

Man has wandered the earth in search of its purpose, for which many scriptures explicitly mentioned "To be with the ONE". The majority of the ancient and religious texts dictate our purpose is to be with the ONE, the GOD, the Almighty. It served them well. We (human consciousness) being part of GOD(the universe, higher consciousness) are just existing for our desires. Desires are the only purpose of our being. We are creators as much as the higher consciousness is. Throughout history, humans are only fulfilling their desires, running for them, running to them and running away from them. It's our only SOLE purpose! The desire for wealth, the desire for health, the desire for conquest, the desire for war, the desire for peace, the desire of destruction, the list is endless. Introspect, look inwards, look no further, why are you moving? It will all come down to fulfilling desires, our only purpose for existence in the universe. We are part of the universe experiencing itself. We are creating experiences with our imagination to fulfil our desires, through which the universe is experiencing itself. The universe's only purpose is to create and experience through the human consciousness. For which UNIVERSE PROVIDES! The ancient teaching condemned the DESIRES as the root cause of all miseries. For which the proponents of the same, DESIRED peace, antagonist of misery.

> *"We are anchored by our desires, it's not us, it's the desires which take us!"*

You, your whole life, were moved by desires! But you are not there yet, yet yearning for the same, but why? Look no further, it's the BRAIN element, which won! It's the limiting belief that reduces your desires in a distant dream, which is not even yours! When was the last time you listened to your heart? When was the last time you silenced your BRAIN? When was the last time when you let your heart its own way? Pickup a desire, I assure you, within a few minutes your brain will start a revolt against it, and it will be reduced to atoms, the dream. For which, the new, reduced dream becomes your desire. Which you eventually get. In the war of heart and mind, the mind always wins, to which unawareness of being, our consciousness becomes a silent spectator.

"The biggest war is the war with oneself, not with the world."

"You are not supposed to change the world, change yourself, and the world will follow."

"All the great changes come from within!"

"It's the greatest SIN to not live according to what you desire. For which you live, which you despise."

One might confuse desire with dreams! There is a distinction! One might use both, interchangeably. But it is not so. Your sole purpose is to fulfil your desires, not dreams! Confusing? Let's shift gears here.

"Dream is an instance of being and desire is a state of being."

The dream is what you imagine and keep it in a distant drawer with no intention of making it in being. Maybe you dreamed yourself about having a penthouse but with no intention of having, it would be just good to have it, if possible. Whereas desire is a state of being, it occupies your mental state, keeps you reminding of its existence, it is housed in your mind. Your dream might be of having a penthouse, but your BRAIN has successfully persuaded you into considering a vast and distant dream, for which you settled for a meagre condo. Now the condo has become your desire, because it is acceptable by BRAIN, as a possibility, now the idea of having a condo has housed itself in your mind and consciousness, for which the universe provides and you end up having a condo. You started with a dream (a penthouse) and desired yourself a condo. This is how you have been living your life up till now. For which I say, you are to blame, you are not a victim but a doer. For which the sole purpose of higher consciousness is to provide you, the consciousness, the child of higher consciousness, because it is through you, the universe experiencing itself. It is the duty, or rather we must say, the desire of the universe to fulfil your desire. We have been dreaming and imagining for gold but settled and desired for silver, for which the BRAIN is to blame, or our untrained consciousness, and UNIVERSE with no affection, fulfilled our desires, leaving us separated from the gold of our dreams. The modern world has engulfed us. We are scholars but yet illiterate in the knowledge of our true beings of existence, we are educated in the workings of the material world but are poor in understanding the workings of our consciousness. For real knowledge, the world termed them as "esoteric". Our whole life we have been trained to work hard and achieve materialism and the whole wide world shunned the so-called "esoteric" knowledge. Where does that leave us?

"You were sleepwalking your whole life, you were dreaming, and now you are aware, wake up to real reality. Reality of conscious living."

* * *

CHAPTER SEVEN

ART OF CONSCIOUS LIVING

The contemporary teachers and "gurus" have adopted a special term for the art of conscious living - "Manifestation" which creates the great illusion, the illusion of "Manifesting" as a tool to achieve material and nonmaterial desires. This further reduces the term to a phenomenon like magic pill, or magic technique, rather than being the essence of our whole beingness. The audience treats "Manifestation" as a tool or technique that they come across to improve their lifestyle, just like keeping GEM stones for good luck. Manifestation is rather a phenomenon of our whole being. The universal consciousness, the higher consciousness is called ONEnss, because all the possibilities exist there at any instance, no desires unmet! There is no void or gap in desires and fulfilment, for which the nature of consciousness is creation, and the force behind creation is desire, which is the purpose of our being. Reduced to just three-dimensional space, where our physical reality exists, there is a void or gap in our desires and creation(fulfilment), that gap, that distance between desire and creation is TIME, which is moving on moments in three-dimensional space. There is no ONEness, for ages, for which the spiritual leaders were pushing us, to ONEness, to that state where there is no gap between desires and creation, for which it is way beyond our three-dimensional understanding of the Universe. Meditation was the "tool" used by sages of our times and spiritual leaders to achieve ONEness. Numerous religious texts talked about the enlightened ones, depicted as meditating in various "Mudras'. Meditation is a way to transcend way beyond our three-dimensional reality. Meditation is the initial gateway to the consciousness of being. Our consciousness is the essence and proof of the multidimensional nature of the universe.

"The Father and (I)son are ONE, but the Father is greater than I."

The quote from the bible perfectly tells the relationship of our consciousness(I or son), to which Higher consciousness is the FATHER. We have inherited the nature of higher consciousness, that is our human consciousness, both are the same by virtue of nature, THE CREATING capabilities. It is our purpose, the desires, for our existence. There is no gap in desires and fulfilment in higher consciousness, there is ONEness, there are infinite possibilities, and all the desires and fulfilment thereof, exist. There is no concept of desires and fulfilment, for which they are already one. Your whole life, TRADERS, you have been choosing your desires unconsciously, you were sleeping, all you need to do it now is choose your desires consciously, and remember, desires are a state of being, your dominant thought.

Let's assume an example of a young girl, which you, the TRADERS, can resemble their past to. The girl, when coming across a rough patch, decides "All men are the same", with negative connotations attached to it. The statement has percolated in the consciousness of the girl. She has made an assumption about the world. Now she lives by it and acts by it, her whole life has a filter now - "all men are the same". She never questions the statement and lives by it, It becomes her natural dwelling state and her DESIRE, remember the DESIRE is the state of being. Throughout her life she gets into relationships, which usually end in justifying the statement "all men are the same". Because it's the nature of our being, the consciousness to create and reflect our desires in the world. She was not conscious of this fact, it was all her creation! TRADERS, now let's take a moment out of our life to introspect our past experiences where we had such moments due to our assumptions. I assure you, once introspective you will find you are full of it!

Our assumptions and beliefs become DESIRES unconsciously which gets reflected in the world by virtue of our consciousness. For THOSE traders, who are assimilating doubts I would suggest they carefully examine their past without any bias, your memory will fail you but not the key, for which it is a law. If your memory fails you, to recollect, I would suggest testing it out. Assume people are always nicer to you, breathe in it, wash in it, boil in it, grow in it. You will find yourself in the midst of appreciation soon.

TRADERS, when returning, you would have two options! You leave with the key or your old garments. The spiritual teachers, metaphysics, always focused on one and only one thing - STATE OF BEING!

""Dare to believe in the reality of your assumption and watch the world play its part relative to its fulfilment." Neville Goddard"

New age metaphysics teacher, pushes on fact - "Universe doesn't give what you ask, but what you are!" The conscious art of Living is the header of Conscious living. If I make a bold statement, you have been manifesting your whole life up till this point. And you were doing it unconsciously, for which we called ourselves sleeping, or sleepwalking. So frequently we were introduced to the personalities and spiritual adages for controlling the mind for success. "Focus is needed to achieve a goal" reiterated by the successful icons of the society. For which we followed the methods unconsciously and lived as such. The world around you, that you are living in, which might be "cruel", "stressful", "hateful", or "tiring", is all your creation of your conscious being. Unknowingly you followed the herd, stocked and bred in the ideas of material achievement through material efforts. The TRADERS got absorbed in so much of the three-dimensional world, that they forgot their true nature of being. Now I call you upon, to introspect your life, the times you face the disparity by virtue of your own assumptions. If TRADERS doubt, which they should not as they came unclothed. I call upon you to test it! You can take a pause on this book of CONSCIOUS living and test it. I still remember my experience, as soon as the wield or my assumption was lifted, the whole world moulded right in front of my eyes! Allow your assumption about any MAN around you, towards you, assume the MAN is the one who adores you, compliments you. When I say assume, I mean assume, without a grain of doubt. You will not fail, for it is a LAW! Sit amongst the brilliants of brilliants! Sit among the riches of the rich! Observe what they talk about and observe their assumptions and the result will be in front of your eyes, their lives! A problem seeker and dweller will be juggling nothing but the problems! Our experience builds our assumptions and the reverse is also true. Assumptions are fortified into our thought patterns and thinking style, which becomes our dominant dwelling state, and by LAW, it is felt! Here comes the role of a referee, the CONSCIOUSNESS. Who is aware of our thoughts? Assume consciously and see the world change.

"The war is not with the world but with yourself!"

* * *

CHAPTER EIGHT

THE CHOICE!

You always had a choice, a choice of experience. But you lived as the slave of your own thoughts. Through thoughts we become slaves, and freedom lies in the same. Go pick a conversation with the people you are aware of, maybe your close ones, friends, or families, it's your CHOICE! And if you ask them, to give their advice to you about life based upon their experiences. Some may say, "Be aware of the world, for it is a fraud!", "Beware while choosing a woman or man, for which they can be evil", "be aware while investing in specific stocks", "beware of your circle", "one should not disclose their dreams before it's fruition", "beware who you trust!", "Only hard work earns money" and the list is countless, I suggest you ask a few. The so-called advice, you might receive, you may think it's their experience and through which they came to these conclusions. What if I suggest, it was their choice! They Chose and assumed and got confronted with it in their lives. With the course of life, the MAN accumulates the experiences and starts building the ASSUMPTIONS around it and with time those assumptions get so ingrained into the MAN, that they become their natural dwelling states, remaining faithful to their assumptions and the consciousness, by virtue of its nature, creates such experiences, which is aided by the higher consciousness.

"AS WITHIN, SO WITHOUT!"

The nature of reality is derived by, or rather we should say, is reflection on our inner world. The reason for careful parenting of a child is emphasized upon. If a child is bombarded with the limiting thoughts of the parents, during the parenting, those thoughts become the world of the child. The consciousness of the child wears the robe of the assumptions made by the child itself. Like father, like son, goes with the same.

When we look at scriptures, we think of them from either a historical perspective or a spiritual perspective. But the author intended it symbolically. With time the intentions and meaning of them changed to mere historical or spiritual facts. One such story is of Abhimanyu, the son of great warrior Arjuna. Abhimanyu was born to Subhadra, the wife of Arjuna. The story goes, that Subhadra, a keen listener of the art of war, mastered the art of war strategy called "Chakravyuh". It was a special war tactic which involved seven tiers of military formations. Subhadra, having heard all the tiers but one, was pregnant with the son Abhimanyu. In the war of Mahabharata, years after, when Abhimanyu grew up, Abhimanyu tore down all the tiers of "Chakravyuh", defeated in the last, all but one. The story is part of the great war of MAHABHARATA. A great deal of spiritualists might take the interpretations under the lens of modern religious connotations. It is all but not this. You can go around and try to find its historical significance, but you will not find any, because it is a psychological drama but not a historical one. The story signifies symbolically, what the author intended to tell us the nature of our consciousness and our higher consciousness. Symbolically, Subhadra represents our own mind or consciousness, Subhadra heard all the tiers of military tactics of Chakravyuh, but the last one, which became a limiting belief! Abhimanyu represents the product of our consciousness, reflection(Abhimanyu) which gets reflected in our world. This has the same limitation as our consciousness(Subhadra). Now you may relate, if your consciousness is impressed by the fact "All is evil", the reality has no choice but to reflect in the physical world "All is indeed evil" if you limit yourself to "I never get good things", the reflection will show the same. The relation between Subhadra and Abhimanyu represents the same relation of our inner consciousness and the reflection of it, the physical world. The state of our inner world or consciousness(Subhadra) gives birth to our physical reality(Abhimanyu) having the same limitations and nature. With the same lens, I would suggest you to take a relook at all the scriptures, each and every fact will send you to the same fact, the relation of our consciousness to the higher one.

Another famous portion of Mahabharatha, which I must tell you. The start of the great war, the conversation between Arjuna and Lord Krishna. Again feel free to find its spiritual or historical significance, for which you won't find any because it's psychological and symbolic. Arjuna on facing the start of the war was paralyzed mentally by the fact that he has to fight his own relatives for a greater good! Arjuna helplessly bowed down on his knees asking Lord Krishna for a way out! The conversation is recorded with great detail in the scripture of Bhagavad Gita, the epitome of all scriptures in Hindu religion. Lord Krishna reveals his true nature to Arjuna on Arjuna's request, for which Lord Krishna says you cannot see my opulence or reality with your mere human eyes and Lord Krishna reveals the truth. The real form of Krishna "Vishwarupa" form or universal form. Chapter 11 of the Bhagavad Gita tells us about this, for which we only understood in the historical and spiritual sense.

Lord Krishna says...

"Behold now, Arjun, the entire universe, with everything moving and non-moving, assembled together in My universal form. Whatever else you wish to see, observe it all within this universal form."

On witnessing the reality of Lord Krishna, Arjuna said...

"I see Your infinite form in every direction, with countless arms, stomachs, faces, and eyes. O Lord of the universe, whose form is the universe itself, I do not see in You any beginning, middle, or end."

Lord Krishna mentions :

"O Arjuna, whatever you wish to see, behold at once in this body of Mine! This universal form can show you whatever you now desire to see and whatever you may want to see in the future. Everything – moving and nonmoving – is here completely, in one place."

When you see the staging of the story. You might see Arjuna, as a warrior and Lord Krishna as his charioteer having 5 horses. Arjuna represents the physical mind of the body having 5 senses (5 horses) and Lord Krishna represents the consciousness. The whole setup is called the human body. The Whole epilogue of Mahabharata is nothing but the representation of our human body and its relation to the higher consciousness. Arjuna on facing his own relatives in war is nothing but a fact : "mind facing his own relatives", doubts and fears created by its own virtue. We live in the limitations and fears created by our own minds. Arjuna asks for help from Lord Krishna, who happens to be the human consciousness symbolically.

And when Arjuna insists on his real nature, Lord Krishna, the human consciousness shows Arjuna his real self, nothing but the Higher consciousness(Vishwarupa form of Krishna). Krishna said you cannot see my real form(higher consciousness) with your mere human eyes. What did Arjuna see? He saw all the creation, all the humans that were ever existed, exist and will exist, all the forms, all the possibilities all the DESIRES, for which Lord Krishna says *"O Arjuna, whatever you wish to see, behold at once in this body of Mine! This universal form can show you whatever you now desire to see and whatever you may want to see in the future. Everything – moving and nonmoving – is here completely, in one place."* Everything, every desire, every possibility already exists in the Higher consciousness, we just need to choose! Arjuna (Human mind), desired the victory of Mahabharatha for which Lord Krishna says...

""Therefore, arise and attain honour! Conquer your foes and enjoy prosperous rulership. These warriors stand already slain by Me, and you will only be an instrument of My work, O expert archer.""

This was before the war even began, Krishna says, your desires are already yours. The whole Mahabharata was physiological and symbolic for which we gave spiritual meaning, and with time its essence got lost. The war of dharma and adharma. Dharma being truthful to your desires, and adharma being - not able to achieve what you desire! The Hebrew root word meaning of SIN is similar to "to miss the mark" but the modern dictionary links it to religious connotation. It is sin, to miss your mark, it is adharma to to not be what you want to be. In the beginning, Lord Krishna says(consciousness)...

""I am mighty Time, the source of destruction that comes forth to annihilate the worlds. Even without your participation, the warriors arrayed in the opposing army shall cease to exist.""

Even without the participation of Arjuna (the mind), it will be done. All you have to do is choose and see how consciousness brings fruits to the world. One must not keep horses away, the 5 horses! 5 horses are significant, for it is mentioned in the scriptures and advised by lord Krishna, one must control the senses, for which it guide the human brain. Remember the staging, Arjuna the warrior is the mind, which directs the charioteer(consciousness) by virtue of the 5 senses. I would strongly suggest seeing the scriptures of our times under the lens of "psychological drama". *"Therefore, arise and attain honour! Conquer your foes and enjoy prosperous rulership. These warriors stand already slain by Me, and you will only be an instrument of My work, O expert archer."* Lord Krihna(consciousness) says, "Arise and attain honor!", which is nothing but a mere expression "Choose what you desire!, assume what you desire! Because it is already yours! I (consciousness) has already done the work". "Whatever else you wish to see, observe it all within this universal form" The expression *"you cannot see my opulence with your human eyes"* implicitly says the things which you desire, might not be visible to you now, but once you close eyes you access your consciousness, which is part of higher consciousness, where all possibilities and desires are all, all the time, at once. This forms the basis of prayers, we pray by closing our eyes and petitioning our desires, the closing of eyes is needed because the desires now are not visible by our sensory eyes, but by our consciousness, for which the imagination is the only language. We speak to our conscious not by words, but by our imagination and feeling.

"Feeling is the secret - Neville Goddard."

The only reason prayers go unanswered is because we use the language of words. It's the imagination and the key to the materialization of our prayers.

"Mathew 7:7

Ask, and it shall be given you; seek, and ye shall find; knock, and it shall be opened unto you: For every one that asketh receiveth; and he that seeketh findeth; and to him that knocketh it shall be opened Ask and you shall receive,"

for which first we have to give ourselves what we desire, Matthew 7:7 perfectly tells us the art of prayers and living our lives. It shows , that one must ask and he shall receive. Ask (imagine and feel) your desires, and you shall receive.

"Matthew 9:29

Then He touched their eyes, saying, "According to your faith, be it unto you."

Prayer by feeling and assuming, you have what you desire and let it be your faith and it will be bestowed on you. Do not petition by words but by feeling and imagination. For which our consciousness receives and goes to higher consciousness and prepares and delivers it to us.

"In My Father's house are many mansions; if it were not so, I would have told you. I am going to prepare a place for you. And if I go and prepare a place for you, I will come again and receive you to Myself; that where I am, there you may be also. And where I go you know, and the way you know." Thomas said to Him, *"Lord, we do not know where You are going, and how can we know the way?"* Jesus said to him, *"I am the way, the truth, and the life. No one comes to the Father except through Me.* Book of John says, I (Jesus, the consciousness) will go and prepare the place for you, which you desire and I will come back again(from the higher consciousness, where all possibilities exist) and deliver it to you, you shall receive! And the father is the higher consciousness. You cannot go to your higher consciousness by your mere physical senses, it's the Jesus in you, that is your consciousness who goes to the Father and brings forth the experience you desire into your world. Throughout time and ages, the messages of the scriptures got diluted into mere historical meanings. Again...

"Luke 17:21. Kingdom of heaven is within you!"

The outer physical world is just a mere illusion and is a reflection of your inner world, thus the kingdom of heaven is within you! Seek the kingdom and it will be delivered to you. But our human tendency is to petition by words and let it be at the mercy of the world, our desires and prayers. The desires are a state of being and experiencing our desires is a choice to be, of being. When was the last time, TRADERS chose to be rich and felt rich? We might desire all the riches of the world by words, but not my imagination and feeling, we feel the poorness in our still minds.

* * *

CHAPTER NINE

ATTAINMENT!

Yraders, you have been waiting a long time! It's time for the attainment of your desires and ways to do it. Lord Buddha at the end of his journey understood the enlightenment and the peace was already inside of him. The desires and dreams were never outside but were always inside of you. We were continuously fighting in our inner world which got reflected in our inner worlds, doubling our sufferings. The chapter of the "Art of Conscious Living" contains the key!

Everything that you desire, you must give yourself first, the wealth, the love, the respect, the home, the job, the place, the peace. Each and everything comes from inside which expresses itself outside. The state in which one dwells inside is the precursor to the state achieved outside, it's not the other way around. A man born in poverty dwells in prosperity inside, the outer world changes itself to the inside of the man. *According to faith, be it unto you* - Matthew 9:29. Traders were wrong, thinking, everything comes from outside, but it is inside which gives birth.

> "*A man is a prisoner of his own thoughts and freedom lies in the same.*"

A man will suffer as long as he associates himself with his body, one must associate himself with his inner being, that is, his consciousness. There is no one but the consciousness. The great war of Mahabharatha represents the victory of dharma against adharma, it is all psychological, but not historical or spiritual. Arjuna represents the mind(physical being) with the help of Lord Krishna(consciousness) riding on this chariot with 5 horses(body with 5 senses) fighting his relatives. The relatives were not in a real sense but were mere subjective metaphors. Relatives, the blood brothers of

Arjuna(mind) are nothing but relatives of the minds, the thoughts. Arjuna(mind), questioned Krishna how he can fight and kill his own relatives(thoughts) with whom he spent his childhood and relatives helped him during the same. The thoughts which served him well, which were the constant companions, to which Arjuna(mind) owes loyalty to, how could Arjuna kill them?

Mahabharata brings our attention to the importance of our thoughts and our hesitation to kill them. To which Lord Krishna dictates the importance of controlling our 5 horses or the senses, which give rise to these thoughts and thus our relatives. I'm sure traders have always seen the great war of Mahabharata under the purview of history or spiritual fact, it is all but not. Another important aspect of the same is reflected in the epic of Ramayana! On the verge of Indian Land, Rama ordered Hanuman, the great servant of Rama to look for Sita, the wife of Rama, who was abducted by King of Lanka, Ravana. Rama sent Hanuman to Lanka, a place Rama never visited and known about. All the sages might point you to the historical and spiritual facts of the epic of Ramayana, It is all but not. Rama, being mind, sent Human(his imagination) to a place unknown to look for Sita(Mind's desire). Hanuman faced adversaries during his journey but was unstoppable because he was all, he was imagination, and imagination knows no boundaries, imagination can go to any place, even if it is unknown(Lanka). Hanuman found Sita in the land of Lanka and returned to Rama instead of bringing back Sita. This is all psychological. Rama being a mind sent his intention, his imagination(consciousness, the Hanuman) to a far land for his desire, through which Rama experienced his desire. The bridge was built by the army of Rama to fight Ravana. The building spanned the entire length from the tip of India to Lanka made up of stones that floated and inscribed the name of "RAM". This was not the real bridge per se, but the symbol, the world produced the way which belonged to RAMA, named and for the RAMA, the world made way only for RAMA to fulfil his desire. If you want to refer to and study epics, feel free and learn all the historical facts and names of figures involved and be spiritual about it, but the author intended to give us real knowledge about the facts of life, but material-oriented ones ornate these stories with great details and diluted these stories. The attainment of one's desire is not different from the attainment of RAMA's desire. One must put his intention and consciousness to his or her desire, send your Hanuman(imagination and consciousness) to your desire (Lanka). The world will produce the bridge, in your name(Ram Setu) over which you will walk to reach Lanka(Your desires). This is the way to attain your desires. One must associate his desires to his own consciousness, not the senses.

> *"An assumption, though false, if persisted will harden into fact. Neville goddard"*

Figure out what you want, what you desire, no matter what it is, don't bar yourself, desire is the motive of life. Make yourself at peace, meditation is the best place where you focus on your consciousness, your inner man, not on your senses, and put yourself right into a situation where your desires are fulfilled. If it is a new home, meditate and imagine with great details you being inside your home, walking down the hallway, opening the cupboard, enjoying the balcony view, all in the imagination, walk as if it's the reality, feel the grittiness of the wall, the coldness of the floor, walk as if its reality. Feel the ownership of the house, plan where you would put the fridge or the TV, all in your imagination. If it's the love of your life, put yourself in your imagination where you are together as you would, but not from a third-person perspective, but from your own perspective, enjoying the food together, enjoying the peacetime along with your beloved one, feeling the emotions you would as you are together, let the feeling run over you. Ignore the senses which tell you otherwise, give yourself the feeling, and feel the worth of your desire. Open your eyes, maintain the feeling, persist in the feeling, and go about your day knowing you have it, what you desire. The world will give you the way to the bridge or the circumstances which will lead you to your desires. It is not your concern whether you have the resources or person to execute your desire, if certain people are required, they will play their part, and the whole universe will conspire for you. You must dwell in the feeling of your wish being fulfilled. Soon you will find yourself on the Setu(bridge) with your name, if persisted. You must follow what Arjuna did, fight your own relatives, your limiting beliefs, your doubts, and your thinking pattern. When you truly believe what you are, you dwell in the state without knowing which reflects in the state of your own world.

> *"Do not prepare for war, when you want peace!"*

Dare to assume your state of being, that is your desire, dwell in the state and the world will find its way to reflect that state. You will soon find yourself in a series of stones floating over the sea of unknown, which will have your name on it and will lead you straight towards your goal. I can assure you, that you cannot have perceived the way to attain your desire, you wouldn't dare to devise the plan, because it was not your concern, your only concern should be dwelling in the desired state.

"The key is your conscious imagination!"

It's the man who once declared he's "good for nothing", and he chose to dwell in the same state, and soon finds himself in the events reflecting the same "good for nothing". He then points to the series of events which proved his point, and found the stepping stones which led him to fulfilment of his desired state "good for nothing". On asking, he will tell you the mishaps of his life, his terrible experiences and giving causes to his external factors, for which he is convinced he is the receiver of the bad news. All this is because he was asleep, unconsciously living. This is life....

* * *

CHAPTER TEN

MENACE

The real menace of conscious living arises from the fact that traders, who have been loyal to their relatives, that is, their thinking patterns and thoughts, which served them well in their past, are hard to kill, just as Arjuna just before the war got perplexed, how he can kill his relatives. For which Lord Krishna (consciousness) said for Dharma one must rise above the rest. This is the time preceding the war, the war with your own thoughts. The biggest war is one with yourself, not with the world. One must conquer their thoughts and senses. The famous imagery of Bhagavad Gita depicts Lord Krishna as a charioteer with reigns of 5 horses in his hands guiding the chariot of Arjuna, while Arjuna is depicted as charging his bow and arrow to the enemies. I welcome you to take my glasses and see this not as a mere factual history, but as a psychological and symbolic one. One must allow his senses, the 5 horses, to their inner being, the consciousness(Lord Krishna) and not be bothered with it, while you, the Arjuna, must defeat his relatives(the thoughts), the loss of control of their senses to their consciousness. For which Lord Krishna said before the start of the war, *"I have already slain your enemies, ... be victorious..."* Giving reigns of horses or Lord Krishna was the act of faith by Arjuna, pondering over Lord Krishna, symbolically the consciousness. One must put faith in his own wonderful consciousness, for which it knows the ways which you could have not devised in the millions of years. The real menace is the victory over one's thoughts! All big changes come from oneself only... Thoughts which served you for decades are ingrained in your mind to the extent that it has penetrated the deepest crevices of your mind. They are your childhood friends. Your desire for your dream home might require a substantial amount of resources, to which your thought would say *"You don't have the resources"*, or *"It would take so and so years to have those*

resources", for which you will succumb to your friend's advice. The friend who is loyal to you has you in your grip, and won't be loyal to your desires. This is the psychological war of Dharma. If you dare to assume and give reins to your consciousness for your desire, the resources will find you. Soon you will find yourself amidst the path where your desires are fulfilled. As soon as you reign your horses to your consciousness, your desires are fulfilled, but one must remain faithful to his desire and consciousness.

It is your consciousness, you must give yourself first the feeling of fulfilment of desire, for which your own consciousness, which is the part of higher consciousness, will conspire in your favour.

* * *

CHAPTER ELEVEN

THE POWER OF CONSCIOUSNESS

The menace is, that you handed over your power to some external sources, idols, clairvoyants, tarot readers, and pundits, who accepted the power and delivered it to you. According to your faith be it unto you... A man who has given his power to a stone, naming it as his own lucky stone, will be powerless and face such in the absence of it. A man who took refuge in palmistry gave power to it and ran blindingly according to it. The power is not in the deck of cards, or the stars under which one is born, the power is you, who chose to surrender his power to them. The report of your stars showing your next 5 years of dreary, to which you believe, you invariably surrender your power and make it your state of being, with each event your relatives(thoughts) supplement the same *"It is meant to be"* becomes your dwelling state, to which your consciousness reflects. Desires are just states of being. And man then points the blame to the alignment of stars for his dreaded situation, living unconsciously. We continuously find the causative source outside of, unknown of the fact, we are the operant power of our own reality. "Because of your belief in external things, you think power into them by transferring the power that you are to the external thing. Realize you yourself are the power you have mistakenly given to outer conditions." Neville Goddard The dictionary definition of faith is "Strong belief and trust" but in whom? External agencies? God? God of scriptures? Scriptures that are nothing but psychological drama, for which we named them, Jesus, Krishna, Rama and the list goes on.... But they were nothing but the symbolism of our own consciousness.

I dare you to look for material proof of the living Gods, you won't find any. We, humans, have a tendency to fill the epics and stories with great details down to the fact of who wore what! But secretly we ignored the implied meaning and symbolism of their stories. We are habitual of ornating the characters of the stories over which we are ornating temples now. The god is not outside, but inside in the temple of our own physical body. The reason for Buddha for laughing incessantly on achieving the attainment was the same, he searched for truth! The truth was inside of him, all the time. I'm assured that Traders want to find the GOD, their own respective god, I won't stop you, look for it, place to place. You will find things which have forms, but not formless, which is God, our own consciousness. I dare you to look inside, define your desires, assume the state, and watch the world deliver it to you. Then you might realize who and what is God! God is your own consciousness. One critical thinker might think the way desires are delivered to him, was meant to be, he will point out a series of incidents, some person or circumstance which made it possible. But that's God's way! The incidents will follow the rules of the physical reality in which we dwell. Real knowledge is not remembering the names of characters of these spiritual stories but from applying the moral of the story, the symbolism behind them in your own life. Your own reality does not exist outside but within, determined by your views and assumptions of it. The relation between the inner world and the outer is of mirror. For sleeping consciousness, the outer world seems to be reflected into our inner world, whereas, the awakened one, for them it's the opposite.

Traders, their whole entire life tried to change the image which is reflected in the mirror, instead of changing which is being reflected, in their inner world. One must change the inner world, the outer world will follow. When one associates itself with the outer world, its circumstances and situations, one must bear the outcomes of those circumstances and when one associates itself with the inner world, the outer world comes bearing the fruits of their desires. The purpose of our being is the fulfilment of our desires, our dwelling state of being, for which the nature of consciousness is the creation of those experiences. Just like the higher consciousness created the entire universe, our own consciousness is responsible for creating our own universe, that is our life. Without consciousness, without an observer, the art does not exist, the universe doesn't exist. "Let there be light", is not a command, not a statement but a desire, which created the whole entire universe. The desire of the higher consciousness "Light", the life of the universe. Let your affair with your own desire be clandestine, you meet your desire when there is no one to see, hear or judge, let it be yours and yours only, soon your affair will give birth to your desires. I see glimmers in the eyes of a few traders lurking in the back, looking for a way to redeem their heartfelt desires. Look no further, identify yourself with your own self-being, your own consciousness, give your consciousness the reality of your desire, and remain faithful to it, you have for long remained faithful to the thing seen, now have faith to the things unseen till they become seen.

When you associate with your external senses, you will breed the doubts and reasons, which is habitual of your being, but when you imagine, close your eyes, just believe in your imagination as a reality and make it your own dominant state of being, your desire. When you see the opposite, remain seated in confidence that you have seen in your imagination, felt in your imagination, thus your consciousness has seen it and felt it. Stand up and fight the opposite thoughts born out of your senses, while remaining faithful to your Lord Krishna, the charioteer, the consciousness who knows your state of being, and remain confident for which you are continuously moving towards your desires. And when you reach your desires, identify who was god all these times. There is Oneness in God, God is one, formless, genderless, directionless, infinite... and description never ends. The majority of scriptures point to that ONE unity, that is god who is all-powerful. But no one knows where he dwells, from where he comes, from where he speaks! Because he is none other than our wonderful human consciousness, formless, genderless, limitless, infinite and directionless. No one could point out where he comes from, because he's nowhere to be pointed at but within us. He dwells in us, creates through and experiences through us. Creation being the nature of consciousness, we create our own experiences and world. Your consciousness has the power to reflect your desires and has always done that, it's the way we have been living but unconsciously. We are always surrounded by our assumptions of things, assumptions of ourselves, assumptions of people, and assumptions of situations, all these assumptions did nothing but moulded our reality as per its nature. If you assume good things take time, good things will find you but after a time, if you assume things always go wrong, they will. Your consciousness is unbiased towards your desires, your wish is its command. Assumptions and thought patterns are the determinants of the state in which we dwell, that is our desire. Desire is a blind father having two sons - Assumption and Thoughts. Father goes where his son goes. You must become the teacher to the sons, a patient teacher, for which the two sons are notorious by birth.

AVIT BANSAL

* * *

* * *

CHAPTER TWELVE

INNER WORLD

We have been too engrossed in the outer world, that we have been focussing incessantly on achieving something that exists outside, this has left man in want! The tenets of Buddhism have marked desires as the root of all miseries. Which is true to some extent. The journey from cradle to grave is nothing but an active play of fetching the desires, but man has tagged desires as the root cause of all miseries. The only purpose, that is of desiring, has made nothing but a sin. Ignoring the fact, yes the FACT, that desire is the only purpose of our existence, through which universe or higher consciousness experiencing itself. Objectively seeing this whole play of fetching of desires, we have given ourselves the outcomes of this play. We, the traders, set our intentions of achieving a desire and on the failure of fulfilment, we reward ourselves unworthy of it, basking *"Maybe it was not meant to be"*. We go again, another desire another reward, another desire another reward, this continues our whole life here. And the collection of such rewards breeds miseries. This whole process happens outside, but we reward our inside, outside to inside, and things become so important outside that we decide to reward our inside. Till a time comes when we no longer desire the things which we truly desire. We start to live inside a world, which is inside of us, where we hold the rewards which we have accumulated our whole lives, this is what we call our inner world. To the unawakened mind, this is all from outside to the inside, the unawakened blames the outside for his inside. Those rewards become our relatives, our blood bonds, our friends and so, we care for them, we don't dare to challenge them and we end up accepting them into our family. The initial chapters of Bhagavad Gita is nothing but a dramatic representation of the same, Arjuna questions his moral duties to kill his relatives for his own desires, to the unawakened mind this might seem immoral. But I must tell the traders, it's not from outside to inside, but from inside to outside.

"As within, so without!"

The whole drama of Bhagavad Gita didn't happen historically at someplace in the past, but it is an eternal story happening within us, all the time. The desire is the cause of all miseries, if we associate the source of desire to be outside, for which the teaching of the great Buddha is aptly correct. And enlightenment is the association of a source of desire from the inside! We categorize each and every event of our lives as good or bad, it is us who give the categorisation to each event of our lives, it is us who give the power. For one the breaking of a vase might be an omen of bad luck, but for others, it might be a good riddance of the same. Just like a maid, we keep our experiences tidy and well-categories in the cabinet(category) of our experiences. It is us who give power and meaning to the events, and we do the same to our thoughts, giving them power! Knowingly and unknowingly we live in the world, our inner world, which finds its reflection in our outer world. The saying "Beauty lies in the eyes of the beholder" is an appropriate example for the same. Instead of paying homage and allegiance to the outer world, turn to your inner world, which is a precursor to the reflection of our outer world. It was never from outside to inside, but from inside to outside. All the great change comes from within It is us who must change, not the world. The cause of your miseries does not lie outside, but inside. The source of our life experiences is not from the man who lives outside, but from the man who lives inside. The source of power which creates our experiences and our reality is within us, and the only thing which creates is consciousness, for which some people call it GOD. As it is from inside to outside, one must live inside as he wishes to be. The bars outside can be melted from within. The desires must be felt within, it is within which creates reality, one must create the world inside of his desire and should dwell inside it. When you give your inner man, who lives inside of your inner world, the shades of your desire, the reality reflects that shade. The feeling of fulfilment of your desire to the inner man is the precursor to the unseen to become seen in reality. The thing that you desire, must be first introduced to the inner man, you must, without any doubt or limitation impose that desire to your inner man, who is none other than your presence of being inside of you. You dare to assume you are the man who you want to be, walk in that assumption, which you hold dearly that it becomes your inner reality, the inner man must walk in confidence, unmoved by the senses and limitations. The unworthiness exists within us not outside, you become worthy of the feeling of fulfilment of your desire, and you become indifferent to the outer world, telling you otherwise, for which you are BRAVE, you live by it. Soon you will find yourself in the opportunity of fulfilment of your desire. If a man wishes to be in love in with the love of her life, he must dare to assume he already is, married to his love, upon the night just before sleep, he imagines his desire, he is walking down the aisle with the love of his life surrounded by the family and friends congratulating them, the man must feel every chatter and love bestowing on them by the relatives on the wedding day, which is nothing than the fulfilment of his desire and he must slumber in such state of being, that is being married, this all should be from not of, he must visualize all these events by being the person but not by seeing himself as a third person. Night upon night, he must give his inner man the feeling of his wish fulfilment and must walk in the day as he is already the person he desires to be. Man will soon find the reflection of his inner world outside, for which it all goes from inside to out. Man must close all the doors of senses and must fight his own Mahabharata, fight with his own relatives(of his mind), that is doubts and fears, it is not for you to determine the ways and means of fulfilment of your desire. For which lord Krishna, your consciousness has already said "I have already slain your enemies, be victorious", you are already married to your love of the life, and be the person you want to be already. Your senses might tell you otherwise because they are perceiving the opposite things as that of your desires, but that's faith! Trust in the things unseen.

> "*And that assumption, though denied by your senses, – though the world would say it is false; if you persist in it, it will harden into fact. This is the law of your own wonderful imagining. Believe it, and it will become a reality.*" *Neville Goddard*"

The Hebrew meaning of the word SIN is to miss the mark, in scriptures its is related to doing of adharma, over which the whole Bhagavad Bita is written, Lord Krishna told Arjuna about the same, it would be adharma to not fight for dharma, he must be victorious over his relatives who stood in from of him and his desire of victory, for which scriptures are nothing but a drama and symbolic representation of the drama, drama of our lives, it is sin to miss the mark, to miss your desire, to miss the person you want to be, that is

SIN of the scriptures. It's the SIN our inner man does, who is no one but us living inside. The things that we give to our own inner man living inside of our own inner world, the same thing we receive outside. It was always this way, not the other way around!

"The kingdom of GOD is within you"

The inner world is an accumulation of our thoughts, our assumptions and our beliefs, together which determines the law of our inner world, to which we call it our dwelling state, and which reflects out to our outer world or reality. The rules imposed on our inner man by ourselves determine the rules imposed on us by the outer world, and this is life. Our inner state of being is nothing but our desires, desire is a state of being which is the precursor of our outer world experience. Man, on its self-declaration of his own worth, sows the seed of its desire to which he reaps in his outer world, to which the bible describes it - kingdom of heaven is inside of you, there is no one to impress but you, no one to judge but you, no one to serve but you. Lord Krishna is not the character who lived in the past in Mahabharata, Lord Krishna was a symbol of our state of being and its affairs, He was never outside, to which we are so habitual to look outside of us, he was symbolic of our own consciousness, which we should seek inside. As long as you seek your desire and God, outside, you will find nothing but miseries. All the great revelations which were revealed, were revealed inside, in the dream, behind closed eyes, not in the outer world, so why did man seek the one who revealed, outside? When man couldn't find it, he built structures, the temple of bricks and placed GOD inside, ignoring his own body being the temple and GOD, our consciousness already inside. We were told there exists good and evil in the world of god, god being all-powerful, but evil does exist! We gave rationale behind the existence of evil which was nothing but a deliberate attempt to justify the presence of evil, but that is not the God. GOD is all-powerful, and impartial, for which he already exists inside of us, totally impartial to our desires, it is us, who creates evil, by desiring evil and goodness by desiring the same. This is the real reason behind the presence of evil. We have ornated the god with the image of humans, which God is not but all. It is us who are responsible for our lives, not the alignment of stars or rules of astrology. Knowingly or unknowingly we are in constant war inside of us, we entertain over 60000 thoughts a day, observe them, you will find the cause of your outer world, brimming of thoughts inside. We quarrel with our friends, families, and coworkers inside all the time, we are habituated to this constant chatter inside of our mind, which shapes our inner world and soon becomes our state of being and gets reflected back in the outer world, but we dare to point our external world as the source of OUR problems, but it was always the inside. We do constantly prepare of our next argument to the quarrel which hasn't happened yet, in hope if it does you will present. We prepare for war in hope for peace and we get war. We desire for peace but prepare for war, it is nothing but an invitation to the war. We are in our imagination, in the constant war with people around you in our inner world, we are arguing with them all the time, right now your mind will be preparing the perfect argument to be used as a rebuttal to a specific person, maybe a family member, a coworker and the list never ends. We term it as an overthinking capability and discard it as a mere act of overanalyzing thoughts. Without knowing argument by argument, we are building our inner world where we dwell in our arguments. We build the world inside and it gets reflected outside and its outward projection, we put the blame on. Man must control his urge to fight in his mind, man is habituated to these urges, like an compulsive need to argue with people, in our mind, no one has power but us, it is us who put words in the mouth of people in our inner world, we feed the word for the sake of argument into their mouths, it is us who prepare for war, no one has power but us in the imagination, but our compulsive thoughts make it so. Man is so ingrained into this outer world that he has forgotten he is also living inside. I would like to ask, the traders, when was the last time you have communed with yourself and has given the inner man the desire of his heart, the inner man is none other than you. We have left the inner man and forgotten about our true nature of being, our consciousness, which is the real creator of the universe, we have been associating ourselves with our outer world, and we have found ourselves completely disconnected to our inner world. This disconnection is the cause of all miseries. The KEY is nothing than the explicit knowing of our true nature, we are the consciousness, a leaflet or child of our higher consciousness, we have lost in the world of flesh, enmeshed right into the atoms of the physical reality, any idea of redemption feels like a distant dream, we gaze far to look for solutions, which lies right inside of us, our inner world and our consciousness.

* * *

CHAPTER THIRTEEN

THE SCRIPTURES

We were told, by the learned man of the scriptures, the GOD who is external to us exists outside of us and guides us. Learned man ornated the GOD with various physical appearances and wrote books depicting GOD as the central character. We ornated gods and presented them into epics and stories to which we call them into our secular history. We revised the scriptures throughout history giving interpretation each time of the respective contemporary thoughts, diluting with each age to come. The scriptures were revelations to us, reminding us of our true nature and relation to the universe, the creator. Scriptures were parables, giving us the revelation of our relation, us and to higher beings. Just like a teacher or a father teaches his own child the life lesson through stories, parables just like Panchtantra stories, using comparable stories and examples like the story of the rabbit and tortoise, giving us the meaning behind the whole story, the characters, in this, rabbit and tortoise, never raced to the finishing line, they were the symbolism of nature of being represented by spirit of rabbit and the tortoise. We know rabbit and tortoise never existed on the same starting line to finish, it was all the parable with an intent behind. The scriptures were the parables, not a secular history, with an intent to teach us the nature of our Father, our higher being. We have mistaken those scriptures which intended to remind us of our true nature of being, mistaken to judge them as historical facts and we ornated them with the historical details and judgements, receding them into just the just epics and sagas. Instead of building our understanding we built the characters, not knowing those characters were the symbols of the intended revelations that our Father wished to tell us, the Father, the higher being. It is a well established fact, the scriptures that we have today have been revised multiple times and now are available in different translations, which have not come to a halt, the learned man is still trying to update them under the lens of modern spirituality. We see spirituality as a different line of path from the mainstream style of living, when one speaks of spirituality we get an image of a saint in the isolation of society and to seek the same we think of going outside of the mainstream system of life, making the dream of becoming awakened a far off, distant concept, and nobody dares to trade into spirituality, for it has become the monopoly of just a few, who are teaching the secular history not the intended message behind them. We are told, in the Hindu scriptures, the battle of Mahabharata, that took place outside on the plains of land in some specific time, and Lord Krishna, the charioteer of Arjuna, the central hero of the Mahabharata. The learned man will date it as an event, the war, happened outside with the great details of the characters. They claim the degree, to which they know about the war of Mahabharata and points outside the presence of lord, the Lord Krishna, which directs us to outside, to look for the lord for the guidance, for which we seek none, when we find none, we create a place to point called the temple, made up of bricks and mortar. The lord, the supreme power is not who can be pointed at, for it is inside of us, the war never happened once or outside, it is eternal, happening inside in each and every one of us. It is not historical, it is eternal. It was not an actual war that once happened on the land of Earth, but on the land of mind, it was a parable intended to direct us to the one who is called supreme. The battle took place in Kurukshetra as the learned man says, and the ancient name of the Kurukshetra is Sthaneswar . the literal meaning of Sthaneswar is "Land of God" "Holy Place", the battle took place in the land of God and the land is our own mind where God lies, our own consciousness which is God! Chariot is none other than our own human body, and five horses, our 5 senses and the charioteer, Lord Krishna is none other than our inner consciousness of being. The beautiful excerpt from the Bhagavad Gita, explains our nature of being, which no learned man will dare to tell you, but they will tell you the dating of the events of Mahabharata.

"prakrtim svām avastabhya visrjami punah punah | bhūta-grāmam imaṁ krtsnam avaśaṁ prakrter vaśāt || 9.8 Bhagvadgita"

Which says, leaning back to myself, I create again and again and again. All which exists, has manifested by my will. "My will", "leaning back to myself", is nothing but about you, These are the words of Lord Krishna, who is symbolism of your own consciousness, the imaginative power, you must turn inside, you are creator of all experience which finds its manifestation outside, the cause is not outside, but in, the Mahabhrat never happened once and outside, it is happening inside of, all of us. As long as we believe the Lord Krishna is someone who is outside of us, there is no salvation, no heaven. He is not who dwells in the temple of bricks, but one who dwells in the temple of flesh, our own body of being. The learned man says, we are punished for the deeds we do commit, out here in the world of flesh, in the outer world. For the unawakened mind, our movement of ours, in the physical world, is punished, but it is not so. The deed that we do inside is the cause, which finds its way to our external world and we are tempted to commit the so-called mistake or deed which makes us eligible for karma. All the good or bad was once inside of us, in the form of imagination, which gets reflected into our own physical world and we commit what we once imagined or assumed to do. It was all once inside of us. It is not that lord Krishna was not inside of us when we imagined the crime, the lord is always there, and the lord is unbiased to us. "Krishna" is synonymous to nothing but *"All attractor"*, an attractor of all manifestations which are brought forward by our thoughts, unbiased to their nature, good or evil. If we harbour evil, he brings evil in our world, if we harbour goodness, he brings goodness in our world, in our lives. So he, the Lord Krishna, is the one who brings what we imagine or assume in our inner world to the outer world. If we live in heaven, he brings forth heaven and if we live in hell, he brings hell, in actuality, the Lord Krishna, who is our imagination or our consciousness of being, is the one who delivers the karma, and he is nothing but one who lives inside all of us! The kingdom of heaven is inside of us, and so is hell. The Lord is not who dwells outside of us or the one who sits above and judges and delivers the karma for our deeds that we do outside. The learned man, who points out to GOD outside, has got the corrupted definition of heaven or hell. Like GOD, the learned man will point heaven or hell outside of us and cause deeds, to outside as well. As long as we believe, The Lord Krishna is one who lived so and so years ago as a man and treat the scriptures as a secular history, we are bound to leave our lives to the hands of our unawakened consciousness who does nothing but run rampant on our intrusive thoughts and assumptions and delivers us the same, for which we believe, the God, hell and the heaven is someone or something outside. The same scripture, in which we are told,

""We behold what we are, and we are what we behold""

implies explicitly the nature of our being, the first part points to our outer nature of existence where the later part, to the inner. It is said in the first part, we bear the fruits of our being, what we are, what our inner world is, which is nothing but a collection of our imagination and assumptions, our outer world is the direct reflection of our inner being. Whereas the later part teaches us about the source, source of our life that we live, it all comes from within "We are what we behold". If you assume yourself to be the victim of hatred, that is what is being reflected in your life. In all, the source is one, it is you. We sow the seed, which we choose, inside of us which grows into a plant bearing fruits and we dare to reason the nature of fruit, the plant bore, as the reason the seed was to blame. The whole wide manifested world around you, your objective reality, is the result of your subjective assumption of life. If you wish to change the fruit, change the seed, for the seed is the cause, not the fruit. We can pick unnumbered scriptures and put it to test, all direct us to one, the one who dwells inside of us, if we can dare to investigate them and understand them as not a historical fact but a parable.

"God is our own wonderful human imagination - Neville Goddard"

We are the only beings who are gifted with speech and imagination, these two are the two sides of a coin, the currency of life. Not knowing we spend the coin in vain, creating, imagining and having imaginary arguments inside of us, we design our own innerworld and blame the outer world for our miseries. As within so without. So we are told time and time again and again through parables in the scriptures, Lord Rama, the exiled king, and his devotee Hanuman. We looked at the story as a historical fact and named the places where they went, and may I tell you it happens all, inside of us. Now we go into the world, ornating each place they went and rejoice in the events which happened nowhere, but in us. The epic of Ramayana is all about telling us the gift of man, Ram who is the epitome of man, the greatest of man as described in the scriptures is a general icon. Icon of man, Ram is man, in the scripture, it is a man symbolizing whole humanity. He found Hanuman, who is a symbol or parable of our human imagination, our consciousness. Ram, the human, the man met Hanuman after Sita got abducted by Ravana and Ram went to seek for her, Sita became the desire of Man, the Ram. Ram in search of Sita found Hanuman, who is the great imagination of man, the RAM, stayed with Ram for the rest of the time of scripture. Hanuman is "Chiranjeevi", one who never dies is immortal throughout humanity, our great wonderful imagination is mortal and never dies. It stays with us, with man, till the rest of our human life. The great epic of Ramayana is nothing but an epic of man, when man desires and he awakens, knowing his own wonderful human imagination as God, his own self of being, his own consciousness, the world is brought to him in the ways no one knows but the God. Hanuman, our own imagination and consciousness of being, brought a whole mountain to the Ram to aid his brother, it is nothing but a message that our own human consciousness knows ways and means to fulfill our desires, the life we want, but for that one has to be awakened, knowing he is the cause of his own deeds, there is no other cause. We are told in scriptures, and you may test it, it will never fail, and the desired once achieved, question yourself, who was RAM all these times, not the man of epic, not the man of past, but an eternal man who lives inside of us, but you may ask, how would I test it the veracity of the claim? Well, turn to the scripture which told us , standing on the verge of Indian continent, Ram sent Hanuman to look for his wife Sita, and soon Ram found his steps on the stones laid in the middle of the ocean, each stone carrying his own name, not of others, straight to the place where he found Sita. For the learned man, it is a series of events and dates, nothing but historical fact. If you dare to assume, which costs you nothing, not a single penny. Send your great human imagination and consciousness to the place where your desire dwells, trust what it tells you, live by it and soon you will find the way , with your name on it to tread upon. You want the material possessions, the money, the relationship or anything that you desire. Suppose you want a well-established business, as the night falls, send your imagination to the place where this desire is true, having an established business. As well sleep in the night, just before the sleep into the moments when we slide into sleep state, close your eyes and build a scene, an imaginal scene where you are the owner of that business, standing in the window of your office, looking down to your employees working for you giving you profits and business, as you imagine, give it all vividness, feel the presence of your employees working for you, feel the ownership of the company. How you would feel knowing you are the owner of such a business, wear that feeling, acknowledge the feeling and see through your mind's eyes, in your imagination and assume the feeling of your desire and become the owner, assume the state of a businessman who is thriving and sleep as such, walk in the day as the person you are, the owner of your business, eat, sleep, think like such. Truly embrace the feeling. Even if your eyes or your senses tell you otherwise, for it is a faith. Faith is nothing but trust on things which are unseen, for which they will become seen, that is faith, the same faith you have been putting outside in the god, put it inside. We are told in the scriptures to have faith in god, and god is none other than our human imagination and consciousness, so put faith in your imagination and trust and believe it to be true. You are the gentleman who is the owner of a great business. Have faith in your imagination, and I know from the experience and from the epic of Ramayana, that soon you will find your steps on the way to your desire, you will be moved to the series of events and opportunities of your fulfilment of desires. And on reaching Lanka to your Sita, your desire, ask... Who was Ram all these times? You can test it and it will not fail you. The only thing that will fail, will be you. You might lose in the war of Mahabharata if you fail to vanquish your relative of the mind, your thoughts, your doubts, and your obsessive thinking pattern. One must constantly fight the war, war with his own thoughts, one might desire a great business, but throughout the day one entertains the thought of having the quite opposite, the doubt on his own abilities, doubt the downturn of the market, doubt of unworthiness, one might also succumb to the inputs of their senses, unavailability of the money, or resources if persisted in your own imagination, even if your senses says otherwise, it is faith. And by faith all is possible, so we have been told the same in the scriptures. One must live as the person he or she desires to be, inside, in his own inside world, the outer world follows. When you walk, you walk in faith, you are walking with the Lord, Krishna, Joshua, Jesus, Hanuman or any god you prefer to say, for in reality it is your consciousness of being, you will never fail, the law, the key will never fail for it is a law. You are the operant power of your own life and reality, it's from you, the life happens not to you. You were sleeping your whole life, pointing to causes outside ignoring the nature of your being. The technological advancement into the new era has diverted your mind from your nature of being, it is the way of life, but we have been living unconsciously all we have to do is live consciously.

* * *

CHAPTER FOURTEEN

THE INVITATION

Now, after all these, I would like to invite you to check the validity of the KEY. I'm sure, most of you must be associated with the concept of the term Manifestation, but it is not, it's not a tool or set of techniques, it's the way of conscious living. Consciously driving your thoughts and desires to its fulfilment. Fighting the war of Mahabharat, where Arjuna(your mind) fights his own relatives(the thoughts). Define your desires, imagine its deliverance in the present moment and live as such, for which I'm sure you will trade soon, the stepping stones to the fulfilment of your desires. Then the traders might want to ask the question, who and what is God! Life doesn't happen to us, but through us. It's always within.

Hope

It's my sincere hope from the readers, that they test the authenticity of my words and may I tell you, It won't fail you, for which it is a way of living. One might feel a resistance with respect to their religious assumptions, for which I would say there is no blissful joy than to realize and experience what our forefathers and authors intended to show us from these scriptures and its real significance. The main intention of writing this book is to share the joy of life and my experience in finding the truth of life and its spiritual significance of it. And it's my earnest hope, that the readers will put into practice and see in the end, that the scriptures were all about us and not about someone who lived in the past. I cannot wait to tell you what bliss and immense joy is waiting for you in-store when you experience this beauty of life.

* * *

Afterword

It is my utmost pleasure to share my experience of this wonderful life with the readers, and I cannot express my feeling of joy, to tell the readers what is waiting for them in the store of life.

Kajal, who brought me to the art of Conscious Living, is my inspiration to write "Possible". She stood as a beacon of life and supported me throughout the journey of writing "Possible". It is my sincere hope, which is unshakeable, to the readers to make use of "Possible" to wake from the dream of life.

It is, only when we awake, we realise it was nothing but a dream! Put it to the test, for which it will not fail, it's the way of living, not subjective but an objective realisation.

My Hope,
Avit Bansal

POSSIBLE

55

Dream The Impossible

9 798896 326373